Receiving Grace

Christian Poetry

David LaChapelle

[7] in order that in the coming ages he might show the incomparable riches of his grace, expressed in his kindness to us in Christ Jesus. [8] For it is by grace you have been saved, through faith—and this is not from yourselves, it is the gift of God— [9] not by works, so that no one can boast.

Ephesians 2:7-9 (New International Version)

POEMS

Led	5	Ending	25
Marching	6	Carried	26
Realization	7	Looking Out	27
Surfacing	8	Doubt	28
Discontent	9	Keep On	29
Restore	10	Opening	30
Leading	11-12	Moving Up	31-32
Growing	13	Cycles	33
Discovery	14	Returning	34
Moving	15	Plead	35
Comforted	16	All Else	36
Counting	17-18	Resolution	37
More	19	Answer	38
Trust	20	On Display	39
Enough	21	Higher	40
Promise	22	Targeting	41
Give Up	23	Test	42
Sharing	24	Journey	43

15 (John testified concerning him. He cried out, saying, "This is the one I spoke about when I said, 'He who comes after me has surpassed me because he was before me.'") **16** Out of his fullness we have all received grace in place of grace already given. **17** For the law was given through Moses; grace and truth came through Jesus Christ.

John 1:15-17 (NIV)

Led

Always wanting

Have enough

The lost is found

Wearing a crown

Led in mysterious ways

Brought to the light of day

Cannot claim for my own

Nothing is on loan

Did not know what I have

Till I came to the end;

Striving against sin

Winded down

So profound

Marching

Cannot get wants

That is a start;

From the heart

Apologize for getting in the way

Break the chains of slavery

Celebrate the liberation

Cease striving for what is near

Now I am found

Love is so sound

Whatever Jesus has planned;

Cannot be all that bad

Trust Him to make a stand

Inherit the land

Realization

God's provision

End of division

Tormented soul

I was on a roll

Striving against sin

My full-time job

Need a revelation

Cannot get what I want

Already have enough

The decision was mine

To leave everything behind

Left undone

The sun

I won

Surfacing

End of the show

No longer on the ropes

Stretched

From one end to the other

There is nothing to shoulder

All His

Knowing me better than myself

Straining to hide

A lost cause

A lost fight

On a ride

Had to burn out

To come to Him

Freedom is to begin

Discontent

The flesh screams

Pay attention please

Immediate gratification

Not long-lasting satisfaction

There is no contention

Just separating sin

Trying to win

Losing battle

Is not my mantle

On course

Jesus will not take me by force

Love is what He is about

No more doubt

Restore

Life's force

Manifesting forth

Illuminating my way

To a better day

Where struggle ceases

Ending my pleading

Trying to earn

What the Lord has already provided for

Unaware of the fall

I need to be small

To stand tall

Humbling myself

Before the Lord

To restore my soul

Forevermore

Leading

Trying to take the lead

When I do not know the way

Creates anxiety

That cannot be kept at bay

Only way to win

Is give over sin

Wanting independence

Pride taking vengeance

That I know better

Then the one who created the weather

Ruffled feathers

Need to settle down

And wear my crown

Gives me sight

To be alright

His case is bigger than my might

To end the fight

Let go

Flow away

From the undertow

That seems so strong

<u>Growing</u>

Wanting more

Does not settle the score

Trusting Jesus' provision

He knows what I need;

Before I need them

A long time to mature

To promote the role

Of believing in Christ

Showing me the light

End of division

Satisfy my longing intention

Kill the fatted calf

I found my place

At last

Discovery

Grace does the work

To let go into the unknown

I can only come so far

Jesus has to lead me,

To the open door

And show me what this is all for

Lost in His love;

Is where I will be found

Crossing the border

To discover the narrow pathway

To faith's bottomless ways

Where I will know;

What has been missing all along

Moving

Will I lose?

If I surrender my life to Christ

Reaching new heights

Out of sight

Out of mind

No time

Take Him seriously or not;

The world is falling apart

The Word tells the story

From beginning to end

It is all Him

My only hope

Something better in store

No matter how far I have come

To the other shore

Comforted

Lord, I need you

To comfort my soul

So, I do not feel alone

Life's struggles seem to wear me down

Refresh me Jesus

To the brightness of your coming

Calling my name

Longing no more

Resting in your loving arms

Forevermore

Counting

Life is a struggle

Why can't I let go of something better

What am I holding onto

That I want to see sown

Anytime Jesus could return

How can I be happy in the meantime

I do not know what I want to give up

All my life I fought for,

Is before my eyes,

Make an identity out of my storms

What did I do for Him?

My life is a testimony

Is that enough

I did the best I could,

With what I had

Nothing more to say

Take me as I am

Anyway

More

I do not have to do it all myself

Not my responsibility

To be perfect in the flesh

I accept my humanity

Letting-go in His loving arms

Cannot stand on my own

Open the door

Show me more

It is not my job

He will finish the good work

Till I come to a point

Where I can be

Trust

Grace is enough

For all my stuff

Cannot carry care

No more

From above

Letting-go of control

Through the open door

The buttons are not there to push

I depend on Him more

Then ever before

Enough

God is enough

His Grace is enough

I am enough

When I depend on Him

Leaving myself behind

There is no time

To stand in line

Cannot strive no more

It is not my job to stay on the road

Comfortable with His lead

Ending my pleading

For another way

To save myself

This is the end of the beginning

Promise

Do not want to be mad

For not getting approval

I craved

Void no more

He has filled the hole in my soul

Validation comes only from Him

I am now looking beyond what I think

Living on a divine plane

Insecurities gone

I am comfortable in my own skin

Settling the scene

I was meant to be me

Give Up

Cannot live the Christian life

Striving against sin

Wanting to work things out on my own

Apart from Him

Has to burn itself out

I need you Lord

I depend on you Jesus

I do not care about my ways

No more

You are not keeping score

Now I know

Your love is enough

Sharing

I cannot will the right

Disciplining myself to obtain favor

It was my pride

I could not shoulder

My wholeness is His responsibility

Not my job to complete this mad discourse

Trying to break free

From this craziness

His Grace takes it away

Like it was never there

From the beginning

Now I am free

To share the love of Christ in me

Ending

Out of the way

Cannot finish the faith

Where did I go?

I am not divided like before

Struggling no more

To save my soul

To fight is over

To look in the rear-view mirror

Down this road of life

Still living

Moving forward

I am all yours

<u>Carried</u>

Your plan is enough

My peace the evidence

In my heart

It is not me

It is all you

That carries me away

Depending on you Lord

To show the work is not mine to ride

That you will complete me in your own time

I settle down and end being restless

That you know better

How to take me to a higher plane

And blessings

Looking Out

I do not know

If I am ready

He is coming back again

Where to begin?

Everything made new

Remember this world

No more

Belief in Jesus

Gets you there

To the other shore

Just how you know Him

The testimony you were

Rewards

Doubt

Heaven is imminent

To face the evidence

Of what we are about

To what Jesus has prepared with love

Eternity is beyond

Anything we can imagine or fathom

Why do I struggle with leaving,

Everything behind

I do not know when that day,

Will come

I guess that is why I doubt His love

How amazing it will be

Keep waiting

We will see

Keep On

Get out of the way

All you need is need

Wanting nothing

Keep waiting

He provides

Just depend on the unseen

To be your reality

Contentment comes,

When you give up

What you are holding onto

It is not your job

To finish the work in you

All you have to do is:

Believe and restart

<u>Opening</u>

Your grace is sufficient

When I am weak;

You are strong

Complain no more

Weather the storm

Crash up the pity party

Dissatisfaction out the door

The remedy is seeing everything,

As coming from Jesus

Christ is the way

The Lord will guide you along

Move on and grow

In His loving arms

Moving Up

Grace upon grace

Increase in faith

Provision provided

Answered prayer

Come forth

Approved by Jesus

Blessings received

Was always the case

Has to come face to face

End the race

Of having our way

Less of me

More of you

Better for all

Ransom paid

We are free to be

Restored

We will see

Destiny

Cycles

When trials come
They arrive wrapped in the,
Father's love
A wandering sheep
To say the least
That needs to be told
Come back into the fold
Our fallen nature
My own way
Hurts on display
Drives me to Jesus
Realizing my need for God
Where I am found again
And have peace
Till the next time around

Returning

When fears arrive

I have strayed from the concourse of faith

Reluctant to need Jesus again

Stubborn as I am

He speaks softly to my heart

This is where peace is found

In my loving arms

You can trust me

I have the best for you

I will not hurt you

Come home

I love you

Plead

When fears and anxieties arise

I know I am a wandering child

Straying off the course

Need to be brought back to Jesus

To have peace again,

And know my place

To realize:

I have been told,

You need me come back into the fold

I will keep you on track

Locked in my grace and love

For Heaven's sake

All Else

I do not know

What you are up too

When I am suffering

It is hard to see you:

As a loving God

Who cares for my soul

I do not know the place

To make me a better man

I cannot make a stand

I give in to you

I do not care

About holding the fort

I have nothing to lose

You won my soul

Resolution

Meet me where I am Lord

I cannot take another step,

Without you

I am listening to what you have to say

Show me the path to take

Lead me into the unknown

Walk with me

To where you want me to be

Help me bring glory to your name

And end this blame game

That is so lame

<u>Answer</u>

I need an answer Lord

For what this is all for

So, I know you are near,

And that you care

That you have not forgotten about me,

And my unsettling ways

Comfort me Jesus

Show me an open door

So, I have something to look forward too

And rejoice in your embrace

So, I can celebrate

Instead of living on the fence,

And end my worry and my ways

On Display

I need you Jesus

To help me cope

To see what is beyond me

Give me something to hold onto

To grasp your majesty

So, I can understand

Destiny unfolding before my eyes,

And ride into life;

The fulfillment of days

Knowing why I am here

To bring glory to your name forevermore

Higher

The sun dawns

It is a new morning

What will the day bring;

Who can say?

What you have planned

Your ways are higher

Then my grading of the lower

Where I see only hurt and pain

Parts of this life

I want to restrain

There is a better way

To follow the Lord's lead

Hope in Christ

Eternity

Targeting

Stability and security:

Evades my soul

I long for it ever more so

You target:

What I trust in the most;

My own self,

My own worth

I plead night and day

You reassure me everything is ok

For when I am weak;

You are strong

I guess you are strong

You are God alone

Sitting on your throne

Test

I am not going to complain

Whatever you bring

I will stay the same

To pass the test this time around

So, I can move on,

Be made strong,

And stay in line

Obedient to you

I try to stay true

You hold the key

To my heart,

And Eternity

Journey

Cannot win

Give up sin

My rebellion against you

To break my stubborn will

You keep the pressure on

Born in me

From the garden

You are the warden;

To give me rest

Freedom is found

In surrendering to you

It is a journey

To come unglued

Worked out on the concourse of faith

Can anyone relate?

I am here;

Struggling with fears

Make my testimony true

Seal the deal for real

ABOUT THE AUTHOR

David LaChapelle is a born-again Christian since the year 2000. David has earned himself two Computer Technical Diplomas from Seneca College, in Toronto, Canada in 1994 and 1996. He graduated with a Psychology degree in 2011, from Trent University in Peterborough, Canada, where he now calls home. David lives a quiet life and enjoys writing and being an author. He is proud of his works, and hopes it will bring him recognition in this life and rewards hereafter. David is a firm believer in reading the Word of God, and the power of prayer and wishes the best for all humanity awaiting the Lord's return.

OTHER BOOKS BY DAVID LACHAPELLE

David's Adventure with Schizophrenia: My Road to Recovery

David's Journey with Schizophrenia: Insight into Recovery

David's Victory Thru Schizophrenia: Healing Awareness

David's Poems: A Poetry Collection

1000 Canadian Expressions and Meanings: EH!

David's Faith Poems: Christian Poetry

Freedom in Jesus

Canadian Slang Sayings and Meanings: Eh!

The Biggest Collection of Canadian Slang: Eh!

Healing Hidden Emotions for Believers

Breaking Clouds: Christian Poetry

Walking Light: Christian Poetry

Let Go: Christian Poetry

David's Faith Poems II: Christian Poetry

Eternity Calling: Christian Poetry

All books and e-books available at Amazon

Manufactured by Amazon.ca
Bolton, ON

40077892R00028